Ship of Bones

'Ship of Bones'
An original concept by Jenny Moore

Illustrated by Can Tugrul

Published by MAVERICK ARTS PUBLISHING LTD

Studio 11, City Business Centre, 6 Brighton Road,

Horsham, West Sussex, RH13 5BB

+44 (0)1403 256941

A CIP catalogue record for this book is available at the British Library.

ISBN 978-1-84886-801-4

Maverick publishing

www.maverickbooks.co.uk

Lime

This book is rated as: Lime Band (Guided Reading)

Ship of Bones

Written by Jenny Moore

Illustrated by Can Tugrul

Chapter 1

Davy the cabin boy stared at the grey stormy waves. He was feeling homesick. It was his third week on board this ship, the *Silver Lily.* He hated the cold wind that whipped his cheeks. He hated the damp, salty air that made his clothes wet. He hated the rats that ran all over the ship, and the swaying hammock he had to sleep in.

Everything on board the *Silver Lily* swayed.

The other sailors said he'd soon get used it, but Davy still felt seasick nearly all the time.

It was hard to remember what dry land felt like now. Maybe that was a good thing. Thinking about his old life back home made Davy too sad. He missed his mum and his sisters. He missed his dog, Rascal. He even missed the screaming baby

next door. But his family needed money for food, and this was Davy's best chance to help them.

"I suppose I'll get used to it," he told himself as he set off to help prepare dinner. "It won't always feel this hard." At least he had Cook's sea stories to look forward to while they worked. They always took Davy's mind off his problems.

Cook had a different story for every occasion. There were tales of pirate ghost ships, steered by spooky skeletons. There were tales of wicked mermaids leading sailors into storms. And there were tales of fearsome sea monsters, like the Kraken. The Gruncher was a good one as well—a two-headed sea serpent with razor fangs. And who could forget the Poisoned Pellicrag, with his venomous spikes? What tall tales would Cook have in store for Davy this time?

Chapter 2

"Ever heard of the Eyeless Ankrapod?" asked Cook, through a thick cloud of steam.

"No," said Davy. He shivered as Cook stirred the captain's stew. "It sounds scary though."

"Scary?" repeated Cook. "The Eyeless Ankrapod isn't *scary*, boy, it's terrifying. It's the most fearsome beast in the whole ocean. It's part whale, part shark, and part giant squid, with twenty long

tentacles and suckers as big as a man's head."

Davy added some more pepper as he listened, thinking about sharp teeth and twisting tentacles. Imagine meeting an Eyeless Ankrapod on a dark, stormy night at sea!

"It might be blind," Cook went on, "but it can smell out its next meal from a mile away. And it can swallow a man whole..."

Davy was so busy imagining that he forgot about the pepper pot in his hand. He kept on shaking as Cook stirred... shaking and shaking. It wasn't until he started sneezing that he realised what he'd done.

“Oh no!” he cried, his eyes watering. “The pepper!” *Achoo! Achoo!*

“What’s wrong with the pepper?” asked Cook, laying out the captain’s tray. “Did you forget to put it in?”

"Er no," said Davy. "Not exactly." *Achoo!*

What would the captain say when he tasted his super-peppery stew? Not even Cook's terrifying sea beasts were as scary as Captain Farshore when he was angry. Davy would rather battle the Kraken or the Poisoned Pellicrag than get on the wrong side of the captain.

But there was no time to make a fresh pot of stew now. Captain Farshore would be waiting for his dinner. Davy crossed his fingers behind his back as Cook ladled it into the waiting bowl.

Achoo! Achoo!

He'd have to hope the captain didn't notice.

Chapter 3

Aaa-aaa-aaa-CHOOOO!

Captain Farshore let out an enormous sneeze. Then another. And another. His face was bright red and his eyes were streaming. He flung the bowl of stew across the table and stood up. “What have you done to my dinner?” he roared at Cook. *Achoo! Achoo!* “There’s enough pepper in there to blow a man’s head off!”

Davy stepped forwards. “That was me, Captain. I’m really sorry.”

“You?” shouted the captain. “You’ll lose your pay because of this, boy. And no dinner for you, either. You can spend dinnertime on lookout duty instead.”

Davy's heart sank. He needed every last penny for his family. And he *hated* lookout duty. He had to sit in the crow's nest, right up above the tallest sail. He felt dizzy just thinking about it. But what choice did he have?

Sometimes I wish Cook's stories were real, he thought as he struggled up to the crow's nest. The rough rope rubbed at his fingers and the wind howled round his ears. *I'd like a sea monster to swallow Captain Farshore.* Just as he was thinking it, something long and red reared up out of the waves in the distance. *Woah! What was that?*

Davy hurried up the last few rungs into the crow's nest. Yes, there it was again. An enormous red tentacle with giant suckers. It crashed back into the water with an almighty splash, setting off huge waves. Davy gasped out loud with wonder.

There was no time to stop and marvel though. "I need to warn the others," he realised, tearing back down the ropes as fast as he could.

But the waves were too quick for him. An enormous wall of water came crashing over the side of the ship. It knocked him off the ropes and dragged him into the sea.

Chapter 4

Salt water rushed into Davy's mouth as he tried to call for help. He coughed and spluttered.

His arms and legs thrashed as towering waves crashed over his head. *Brrr.* The sea was icy cold and Davy had never been much of a swimmer. But somehow he managed to stay afloat. He just hoped the fearsome monster he'd spotted was headed in the other direction.

By the time the huge waves had cleared, the ship had gone too, swallowed up by the mist. Davy's heart sank. Much as he'd hated life on the ship, he'd give anything to be back there now.

Suddenly he saw what looked like a ship's shadow looming out of the rain. It was heading this way. Was it the *Silver Lily* coming back for him?

Davy squinted through the mist. No, this ship was white and wispy-looking, with dark sails... dark sails and a grinning skull and crossbones flag flying from the mast. It was like the pirate ghost ship from Cook's stories!

"Ahoy there," came a low growly voice. A skeleton in a pirate hat leaned over the side of the ship.

Davy blinked in disbelief. Monsters... ghost ships... skeleton pirates... Were *all* of Cook's stories true?

"Grab hold of my hand," said the skeleton, "and I'll pull you in."

Davy did as he was told, grateful to be out of the freezing water.

"Hurry now," said the skeleton. "I've got a monster to catch."

Chapter 5

"The name's Captain Scarbone," said the pirate, handing Davy a dry blanket. "And I'm looking for the Eyeless Ankrapod... a fearsome monster with twenty tentacles and suckers as big as a man's head."

"I-I-I know the one you mean," said Davy. His teeth were chattering and he was shaking all over. "But why do you want to find it?"

“Because it took my crew and swallowed them whole,” said Captain Scarbone. “I’m doomed to chase the Eyeless Ankrapod and get my revenge. But I’m close now. I can feel it in my bones.”

"I saw a giant red tentacle when I was on lookout duty," Davy told him. "It was huge."

The pirate nodded. "That'll be him," he growled. "He'll be sniffing out his next meal. There's no meat on *these* old bones, but with any luck the smell of fresh cabin boy will lead him straight to us."

Davy gulped. *The smell of fresh cabin boy?* He felt like a worm, wiggling helplessly on the end of a fishing line. His legs shook harder than ever as the pirate handed him a telescope.

"Come on, you miserable monster," roared Captain Scarbone. He shook his fist at the waves.

"Come and finish what you started. We're ready for you."

I'm not ready, thought Davy. It was too late to back out now though. He peered through the telescope, hoping the monster had changed its mind. But there it was... an enormous red beast, rearing up out of the water in a tangle of tentacles.

Chapter 6

"You take the wheel," Captain Scarbone ordered. "I'll man the guns. Turn the ship to starboard and hold her steady."

"What? You're leaving me to steer the ship?" asked Davy. "But I don't know how..."

It was too late to argue though. The pirate had already gone. Davy tugged at the wheel with all his might. Yes, it was working... the ship was turning.

The ship's guns were aimed right at the eyeless monster now. Would they be enough to stop him?

BOOM! The first cannonball soared through the air.

SMASH! It hit the monster's sharp steely teeth and shattered.

BOOM! SHATTER!
BOOM! SHATTER!

It was no good. Cannonball after cannonball smashed into pieces against the monster's jaws. The Eyeless Ankrapod was unstoppable!

There was a loud howl of despair from below deck. Davy left the wheel and hurried down to investigate.

Captain Scarbone was sat with his skull in his hands. "It's no good," he cried. "Nothing can defeat a monster like that. I'll never get my revenge now."

But Davy had an idea. It was a wild, crazy idea, but it was worth a try. It was either that or get eaten by the Ankrapod!

"Which way to the kitchen?" he asked.

Chapter 7

"The kitchen?" roared Captain Scarbone. "How can you think about food at a time like this? *We're* the ones who'll be dinner when that monster reaches us." But Davy explained his idea and the pirate grinned. "Genius! We'll have to hurry though," he said.

Captain Scarbone tore off to the kitchen and returned with a small wooden casket. A casket filled with pepper! They loaded it into the cannon in place of a cannonball and got ready to fire.

"We've only got one chance at this," said Davy, "so we can't fire too soon."

They watched through the gun hole. The Eyeless Ankrapod was gaining on them fast now. Closer and closer it came. Its jaws stretched open, ready to bite. Closer and closer...

"Fire!"

BOOM! The casket of pepper flew through the air towards the monster's open mouth. It shattered on its steely teeth, releasing a thick black cloud of pepper.

The monster let out an almighty **ROAR...**

followed by an enormous sneeze. *Lots* of sneezes!

AAA-CHOOOO! Out flew a ship's mast, with a tattered sail still attached.

AAA-CHOOOO! AAA-CHOOOO!

Out flew a rowing boat and a collection of swords.

AAA-CHOOOO! AAA-CHOOOO!

AAA-CHOOOO! Out flew a treasure chest and Captain Scarbone's skeleton crew. The monster swam off, still sneezing.

Captain Scarbone slapped Davy on the back and cheered. "We did it! I mean *you* did it. I reckon that pepper knocked out his sense of smell too."

"You mean we're safe now?" asked Davy.

"Safe and rich," said the pirate. "It looks like I've got my missing treasure back as well as my crew!"

Chapter 8

"This is for you," said Captain Scarbone, handing Davy a treasure chest. "To say thank you for saving my crew."

Oof!

The chest was so heavy, Davy could barely lift it. He stared at the glittering treasure inside. There was enough there to look after his family for years...

"And we'll try and catch up that ship of yours," said the pirate. "So you can re-join *your* crew."

Davy shook his head. "I'd rather have a lift back to port if that's alright. I've had enough sea adventures to last me a lifetime!"

"What? You mean you don't want to see the Gruncher or the Poisoned Pellicrag?" Captain Scarbone grinned. "Or the singing mermaids?"

"The only thing *I* want to see is dry land and a nice warm bed," said Davy.

***

Davy's legs still felt strange after so long at sea. The ground seemed to rock and sway beneath him as he trudged towards his house, his chest bumping against his shoulder. The pirate gold grew heavier with every step, but Davy's heart had never felt lighter.

"No more lookout duty or scrubbing the deck for me," he told a passing bird. "And no more monsters."

There was a loud growling noise as he reached the garden gate. Davy jumped. Maybe he'd spoken too soon.

But the growls gave way to high-pitch whines of excitement. A large brown dog came bounding out of the door, closely followed by Davy's family.

"Rascal!" cried Davy, burying his face in his dog's soft fur. "I missed you, boy. I missed you all," he added, wiping away a happy tear.

"You'll never believe the adventures I've had. I've got so much to tell you."

Discussion Points

1. What is the one thing Davy likes about life on the *Silver Lily*?

2. Who ruins Captain Farshore's dinner?

a) Cook

b) Davy

c) Captain Scarbone

3. What was your favourite part of the story?

4. Why is Captain Scarbone looking for the Eyeless Ankrapod?

5. How else do you think Davy and Captain Scarbone could have stopped the sea monster?

6. Who was your favourite character and why?

7. There were moments in the story when Davy had to **make decisions quickly**. Where do you think the story shows this most?

8. What do you think happens after the end of the story?

Book Bands for Guided Reading

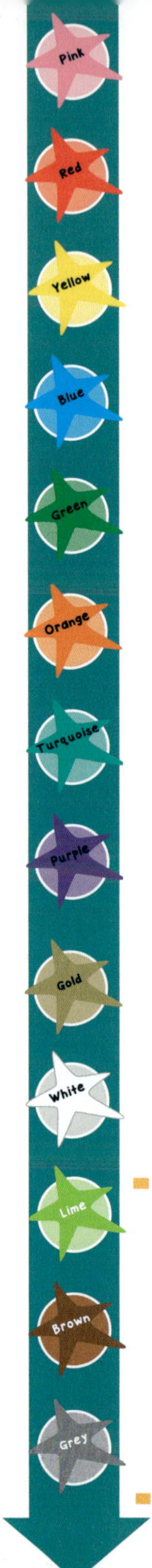

The Institute of Education book banding system is a scale of colours that reflects the various levels of reading difficulty. The bands are assigned by taking into account the content, the language style, the layout and phonics. Word, phrase and sentence level work is also taken into consideration.

The Maverick Readers Scheme is a bright, attractive range of books covering the pink to grey bands. All of these books have been book banded for guided reading to the industry standard and edited by a leading educational consultant.

To view the whole Maverick Readers scheme, visit our website at

www.maverickearlyreaders.com

Or scan the QR code to view our scheme instantly!

Maverick Chapter Readers

(From Lime to Grey Band)

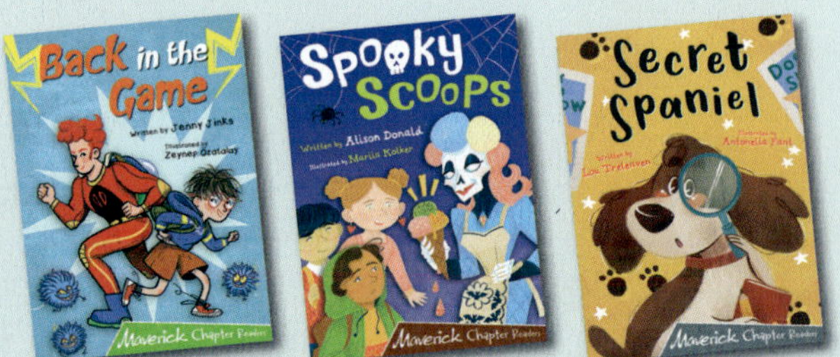